# French to learn be
(or whilst on holiday)

GH00870269

Essential words for your

# Challenges to speak French on holiday
How many of the challenges can you complete?

# Are you going to France soon?

If you have booked a holiday to France, or you are thinking of going to France soon, then that's very e x c i t i n g !  France is a lovely country, and holidays in France are such a special and wonderful experience.

In France, the people speak French.  I always find it fun speaking French when I go to France.   Why don't you try and learn some French words and phrases before you go?

In the first section of this book there are lots of fun activities to do to help you learn some French. And then when you are in France, see how many of the 15 challenges from the second part of this book that you can complete.

Bonjour!
Je m'appelle Anne.

Answer Anne in French by writing:
**Bonjour, Je m'appelle** (Hello, my name is)
Then write your own name:

_____ , _____ _____ _____ .

# Essential words

| | |
|---|---|
| Bonjour ............... | Hello (daytime) |
| Bonsoir ............... | Good evening |
| Au revoir ............... | Good bye |
| oui ...................... | yes |
| non .................... | no |
| s'il vous plaît .......... | please |
| merci .................... | thank you |

Circle the following in the oval shape below:

Bonjour       Bonsoir       Au revoir

oui   non       merci       s'il vous plaît

xde(oui)yins'ilvousplaîtrewBonjourtxA
revoirlkphmerciplknonixBonsoirpe

Follow the lines to see what the children are saying. Write what each child is saying:

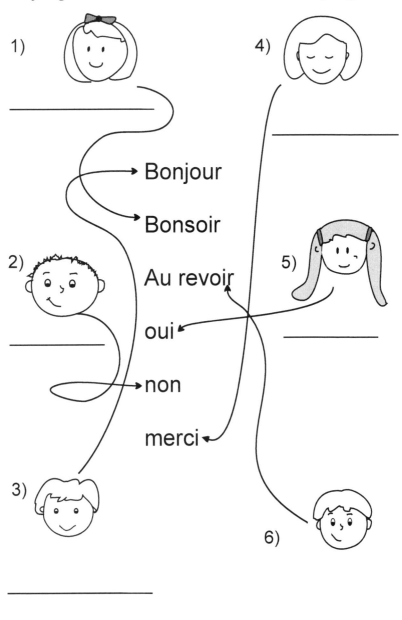

1) _____

4) _____

Bonjour

Bonsoir

2) _____

Au revoir

5) _____

oui

non

merci

3) _____

6) _____

# Match the French and the English words:

Bonjour

please

hello

oui

s'il vous plaît

no

yes

non

merci

Good bye

Au revoir

thank you

# Les numéros

**10**
dix

**7**
sept

**8**
huit

**9**
neuf

**4**
quatre

**5**
cinq

**6**
six

**1**
un

**2**
deux

**3**
trois

# How many ice creams are there?

(Write your answers in French)

1 = un        2 = deux   3 = trois

4 = quatre   5 = cinq

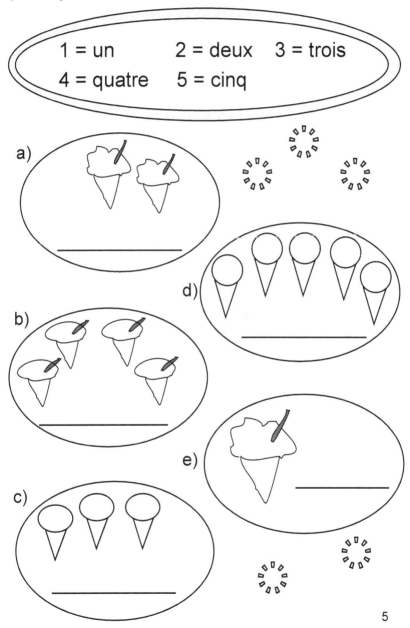

a) _____

b) _____

c) _____

d) _____

e) _____

5

# Draw the correct number of sand castles:

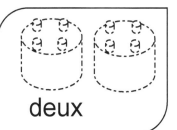

deux

1 = un
2 = deux
3 = trois
4 = quatre
5 = cinq

a)

quatre

b)

un

c)

trois

d)

cinq

# a) Write the following numbers with the smallest number first:

(dix is the largest number so will be last.)

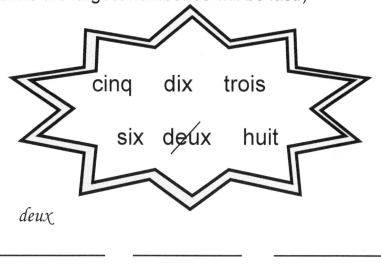

cinq    dix    trois

six   deux    huit

*deux*

_____      _____      _____

_____      _____      _____

# b) Which four numbers between 1 & 10 are missing?

_____      _____

_____      _____

# Les boissons froids

(cold drinks)

un coca

un coca light

un Orangina

une limonade

un jus d'orange

une eau minérale

# What drink is it?

Write what the drinks are called in French:

| un coca | un coca light | un jus d'orange |
| un Orangina | une limonade | une eau minérale |

1)

_____

2)

_____

3)

_____

4)

_____

5)

_____

6)

_____

# What drinks do you like?

Write your favourite drink first, then write the other drinks in **order of preference**.
The drink you like least should be last.

| un coca | un coca light | un jus d'orange |
| un Orangina | une limonade | une eau minérale |

Favourite drink:

_____

_____

_____

_____

_____

Least favourite drink:

_____

# Lets order some drinks!

Draw a line between the drink and the person asking for the drink:

Je voudrais un coca, s'il vous plaît

une eau minérale, s'il vous plaît

Je voudrais une limonade, s'il vous plaît

un jus d'orange, s'il vous plaît

un Orangina, s'il vous plaît

Notice that to order a drink, you could say:

a drink followed by **s'il vous plaît.**
(s'il vous plaît means please)

or

**Je voudrais**, then a drink & **s'il vous plaît**.
(Je voudrais means I would like)

11

# Les boissons chauds

(hot drinks)

un thé

un café

| | |
|---|---|
| un thé au lait ………. | a tea with milk |
| sans lait ……………. | without milk |
| un café au lait ……… | a coffee with milk |
| un café noir ………… | a black coffee |
| grand ………………. | big |
| petit …………………. | small |

# Match the French and the English phrases:

un grand café

un grand thé

a big coffee

un thé au lait

a big tea

a tea with milk

un café noir

un petit café

a small coffee

a black coffee

13

# Au café (At the café)

Read what the customers are ordering:

un grand café noir

Marie

un grand thé au lait

Anne

un petit café au lait

Marc

un peitit thé sans lait

Sophie

un grand thé au lait

Luc

Pierre

un petit café noir

Look at what drinks the people want on the page opposite. Complete the table:

|        | small | big | tea | coffee | milk |
|--------|-------|-----|-----|--------|------|
| Marie  |       | ✓   | ✓   |        | ✗    |
| Anne   |       |     |     |        |      |
| Marc   |       |     |     |        |      |
| Sophie |       |     |     |        |      |
| Luc    |       |     |     |        |      |
| Pierre |       |     |     |        |      |

# Food

 des **frites** (chips)

 du **poulet** (chicken)

 du **jambon** (ham)

 du **fromage** (cheese)

 des **champignons** (mushrooms)

 de la **salade** (salad)

Look at the page opposite, and draw the following things:

des champignons

des  frites

de la salade

du fromage

du jambon

du poulet

# Au restaurant

In France, the prices on menus will be in euros.
The euro sign looks like this: €

Look at the menu below.  Write in the space below
what you would like to have in the restaurant:
(avec = with      et = and)

---

## MÉNU

Poulet ...........................................€  8

Hamburger ...............................€  6

Hamburger avec fromage ............€  7

Pizza (jambon et champignons).......€  9

Frites .......................................€  3

Salade ....................................€  2

Look at the menu on the page opposite.
How much do the following things cost?
Write your answers in French:

1) chips _____ euros

2) chicken _____ euros

3) salad _____ euros

1 = un
2 = deux
3 = trois
4 = quatre
5 = cinq
6 = six
7 = sept
8 = huit
9 = neuf
10 = dix

4) ham & mushroom pizza _____ euros

5) hamburger with cheese _____ euros

6) hamburger and chips _____ euros

7) chicken and salad _____ euros

# La boulangerie (the baker's)

Copy the French words for some things you will see in a French bakery:

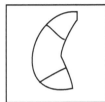 un croissant (a French pastry)

_____

 une baguette (French stick)

_____

 du pain (bread)

_____

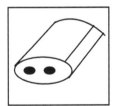 un pain au chocolat
(a French pastry with chocolate inside)

_____

 un gâteau (a cake)

_____

# Croissants

Croissants are made with sweet flaky pastry dough, so they are light and flaky.

How many croissants are there in each box?:

a)
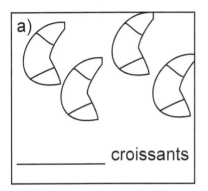
_____ croissants

b)
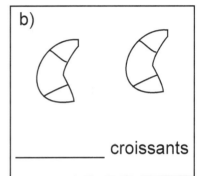
_____ croissants

c)
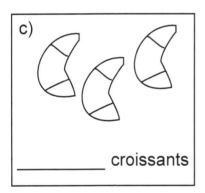
_____ croissants

d)
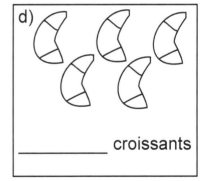
_____ croissants

| 1 = un | 2 = deux | 3 = trois |
|---|---|---|
| 4 = quatre | 5 = cinq | |

# Pains au chocolat

A pain au chocolat is similar to a croissant, but it has chocolate inside. It's very tasty!

Count how many pains au chocolat there are, and write the number in French:

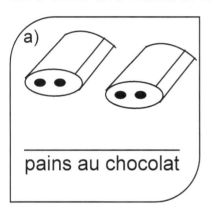

a)

_____
pains au chocolat

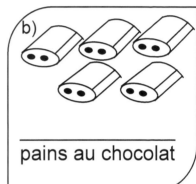

b)

_____
pains au chocolat

c)

_____
pains au chocolat

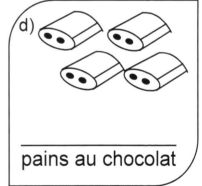

d)

_____
pains au chocolat

| | | |
|---|---|---|
| 1 = un | 2 = deux | 3 = trois |
| 4 = quatre | 5 = cinq | |

# Bakery shopping!

2 = deux
3 = trois
4 = quatre

Draw the following things in the bag:

deux baguette**s**          trois croissant**s**

deux gâteau**x**          quatre pain**s** au chocolat

 Notice the endings for the food have either an s or an x when there is more than one. ⭐

# Les glaces

Read the French words and colour the ice creams:

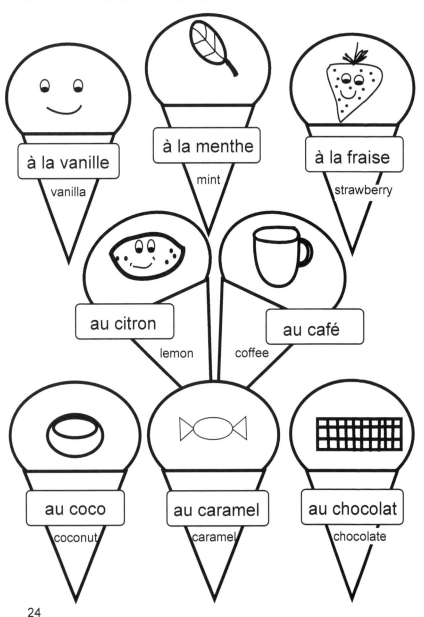

à la vanille
vanilla

à la menthe
mint

à la fraise
strawberry

au citron
lemon

au café
coffee

au coco
coconut

au caramel
caramel

au chocolat
chocolate

# Ice creams

Match the French with the English meaning:

à la menthe

mint

à la fraise

lemon

strawberry

à la vanille

au citron

au coco

coconut

vanilla

caramel

au caramel

coffee

chocolate

au café

au chocolat

# Une glace (an ice cream)

Draw your favourite ice cream, and label it in French:

# Une glace, s'il vous plaît

Ask for the following ice creams:

1) une glace ___ _____, s'il vous plaît

2) une glace __ ___ _____, s'il vous plaît

3) une glace __ _____, s'il vous plaît

4) ____ _____ ___ _____,
s'il vous plaît

5) ____ _____ __ __ _____,
s'il vous plaît

6) ____ _____ ___ _____,
____ _____ _____

| à la fraise | au coco | au chocolat |
|---|---|---|
| à la menthe | au café | au citron |

# Souvenirs

un ballon

un t-shirt

un stylo

un nounours

une gomme

un crayon

Which of the above would you like to buy
as a holiday souvenir?
(Write the French for any souvenirs you would like)

_____

_____

# What is it?

Draw a line from the picture to the French word:

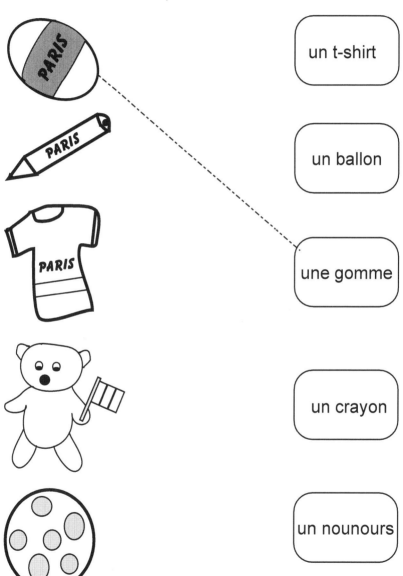

un t-shirt

un ballon

une gomme

un crayon

un nounours

#  Souvenirs

Draw the following things:

1)

un nounours

2)

un t-shirt

3)

un ballon

4)

un crayon

un t-shirt = a t-shirt    un crayon = a pencil

un ballon = a ball    un nounours = a teddy

# Au magasin (At the shop)

Ask for the following things:

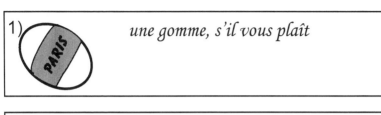

*une gomme, s'il vous plaît*

# Postcards & stamps

Postcards can be nice to buy either as a souvenir of your holiday, or to send to someone you know.

## une carte postale
(a postcard)

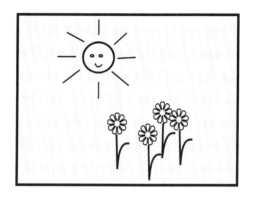

un timbre pour Grand Bretagne

(a stamp for Great Britain)

un timbre pour les Étas Unis

(a stamp for America)

un timbre pour Europe

(a stamp for Europe)

# Combien? 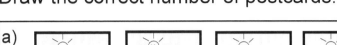 (How many?)

Draw the correct number of postcards:

**a)**

quatre cartes postales

**b)**

deux cartes postales

**c)**

cinq cartes postales

**d)**

trois cartes postales

1 = un   2 = deux   3 = trois   4 = quatre   5 = cinq

# A French town

Draw some trees in the town
as you read the French words:

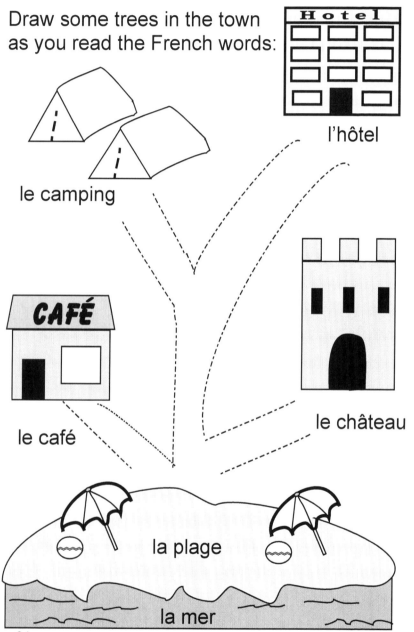

l'hôtel

le camping

CAFÉ

le café

le château

la plage

la mer

# Places in a town

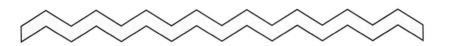

Look at the page opposite.  How do you say
the following in French?:

1) The beach          _____

2) The sea            _____

3) The campsite       _____

4) The café           _____

5) The hotel          _____

6) The castle         _____

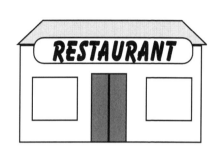

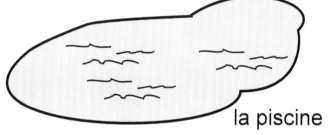

la piscine

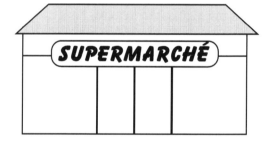

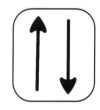

ascenseur

les toilettes

les douches

Look at the page opposite.  Draw a line between the French and the English words:

le magasin                           the swimming pool

les toilettes                        the restaurant

le restaurant                     the shop

le supermarché                the lift

les douches                     the toilets

la piscine                          the supermarket

l'ascenseur                     the showers

# Answers

## Page 1

x de oui vin s'ilvousplaître w Bonjour tx
(circular word-search solution containing: oui, s'ilvousplaît, Bonjour, Au revoir, Bonsoir, non, merci)

## Page 2

1) Bonsoir   2) non   3) Bonjour
4) merci   5) oui   6) Au revoir

## Page 3

Bonjour = hello   s'il vous plaît = please   oui = yes
merci = thank you   non = no   Au revoir = Good bye

## Page 5

a) deux   b) quatre   c) trois   d) cinq   e) un

## Page 6

The correct number of sand castles is as follows:
a) 4   b) 1   c)3   d) 5

## Page 7

a) deux   trois   cinq   six   huit   dix

b) un   quatre   sept   neuf

## Page 9

1) un jus d'orange
2) une limonade
3) un coca light
4) une eau minérale
5) un Orangina
6) un coca

## Page 11

## Page 14

un grand café = a big coffee
un grand thé = a big tea
un thé au lait = a tea with milk
un café noir = a black coffee
un petit café = a small coffee

|        | small | big | tea | coffee | milk |
|--------|-------|-----|-----|--------|------|
| Marie  |       | ✓   |     | ✓      | ✗    |
| Anne   |       | ✓   | ✓   |        | ✓    |
| Marc   | ✓     |     |     | ✓      | ✓    |
| Sophie | ✓     |     | ✓   |        | ✗    |
| Luc    |       | ✓   | ✓   |        | ✓    |
| Pierre | ✓     |     |     | ✓      | ✗    |

## Page 17

des champignons = mushrooms    des frites = chips
de la salade = salad        du fromage = cheese
du jambon = ham            du poulet = chicken

## Page 19

1) trois euros    2) huit euros    3) deux euros
4) neuf euros    5) sept euros    6) neuf euros
7) dix euros

## Page 21

a) quatre    b) deux    c) trois    d) cinq

## Page 22

a) deux    b) cinq    c) trois    d) quatre

40

## Page 23

The following should be drawn in the bag:

2 French sticks,  3 croissants,  2 cakes
4 pains au chocolat

## Page 25

à la menthe = mint          à la fraise = strawberry
au citron = lemon           à la vanille = vanilla
au coco = coconut           au caramel = caramel
au café = coffee            au chocolat = chocolate

## Page 27

une glace au café, s'il vous plaît
une glace à la fraise, s'il vous plaît
une glace au citron, s'il vous plaît
une glace au coco, s'il vous plaît
une glace à la menthe, s'il vous plaît
une glace au chocolat, s'il vous plaît

## Page 29

a rubber = une gomme    a pencil = un crayon
a t-shirt = un t-shirt      a teddy bear = un nounours
a ball = un ballon

## Page 30

The following things should be drawn:

1) a teddy bear   2) a t-shirt   3) a ball   4) a pencil

## Page 31

1) une gomme, s'il vous plaît
2) un t-shirt, s'il vous plaît
3) un crayon, s'il vous plaît
4) un ballon, s'il vous plaît
5) un nounours, s'il vous plaît
6) un stylo, s'il vous plaît

## Page 33

The number of post cards drawn should be:

a) 4    b) 2    c) 5    d) 3

## Page 35

1) la plage    2) la mer    3) le camping
4) le café    5) l'hôtel    6)  le château

## Page 37

la piscine = the swimming pool
les toilettes = the toilets
le restaurant = the restaurant
le supermarché = the supermarket
les douches = the showers
le magasin = the shop
l'ascenseur = the lift

# Challenges to speak French on holiday

The next part of this book contains various challenges to speak French whilst in France.

It's so nice speaking French, so it's going to be fun!

The challenges are flexible, so for the challenges containing food, if you don't eat any of the things outlined in the challenges, then you can change the challenge to something else.

On many of the challenge pages there is an alternative challenge, but if you prefer you can think of your own alternative challenge.

Tick the target achieved box when you have completed the challenge. How many of the challenges can you do?

Greeting challenge 1: Can I say hello in French?

To complete this challenge you need to say hello to **at least 5 people**.

Useful phrases:

Hello (when it's day time):  **Bonjour**

Hello (when it's evening):  **Bonsoir**

If you want to, you can tick the number of times you say the following:

Bonjour

Bonsoir

Bonjour

**Challenge achieved**

Tick when completed

Greeting challenge 2: Can I say goodbye in French?

To complete this challenge you need to say goodbye to **at least 5 people**.

To say goodbye say : **Au revoir**

If you want to, you can tick the number of times you say goodbye in the oval shape below:

Au revoir

**Challenge achieved**

Tick when completed

## Can I say thank you in French?

To complete this challenge you need to say thank you in French **at least 5 times.**

To say thank you in French say **merci**

Challenge yourself further and see how many times you can say merci during your holiday. You can tick the box below each time you say merci:

How many times did you manage to say merci during your holiday?
_____ times

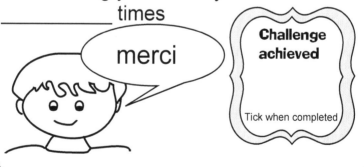

merci

Challenge achieved

Tick when completed

## Can I ask for a drink in French?

To complete this challenge, you need to ask for a drink of your choice in French.

Remember to say **s'il vous plaît** (please)
e.g.une limonade, s'il vous plaît
(a lemonade, please)

un orangina

un coca

une eau minérale

une limonade

un jus d'orange

un coca light
(diet coke)

**Challenge achieved**

Tick when completed

## Can I ask for an ice cream in French?

If you like ice creams, then challenge yourself to order one in French!!
(Choose your favourite flavour or flavours)

### Useful phrases:

une glace .............. an ice cream

au chocolat ............ chocolate

à la fraise .............. strawberry

et......................... and

à la vanille .............. vanilla

s'il vous plaît .......... please

See page 24 for additional flavours

une glace au chocolat, s'il vous plaît

**Challenge achieved**

Tick when completed

alternative challenge:
buy some strawberries:
**des fraises, s'il vous plaît**

## Can I buy something from a bakery in French?

In France there are lots of delicious bakeries selling tasty things. To complete this challenge, ask for for one or more of the following:

une baguette

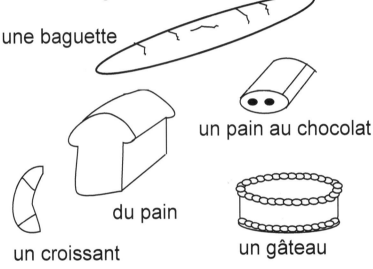

un pain au chocolat

du pain

un croissant

un gâteau

Remember to say **s'il vous plaît** after what you ask for

_____

alternative challenge: ask for some cheese:
**du fromage, s'il vous plaît**

**Challenge achieved**

Tick when completed

## Can I order a pancake in French?

One of the many specialities of France is a pancake, so why don't you try one and order it in French.

**Useful phrases**

une crêpe ...............a sweet pancake

au sucre ................. with sugar

une galette ............. a savoury pancake

au jambon .............. with ham

et ..........................and

au fromage ............. with cheese

s'il vous plaît ...........please

Alternative challenge
Ask for an orange juice:
**un jus d'orange,
s'il vous plaît**

Challenge achieved

Tick when completed

## Can I ask for a table in French?

If you are going out for a drink or to eat, why don't you ask for a table in French?

**Useful phrases**

une table, s'il vous plaît … a table, please

Or say how many you want the table for:

une table pour trois personnes,
s'il vous plaît   (a table for three, please)

une table pour quatre personnes,
s'il vous plaît   (a table for four, please)

1 … … un
2 …… deux
3 …… trois
4 …… quatre
5 …… cinq
6 …… six
7 …… sept
8 …… huit

Challenge achieved

Tick when completed

Can I order some food in French?

For this challenge you need to go to a French café or restaurant and order something in French.

Write on the line below what you order:

_____

Remember to say **s'il vous plaît (**please) after whatever you order.

e.g.    du poulet, des frites et de la salade, s'il vous plaît

**Challenge achieved**

Tick when completed

## Can I ask for the bill in French?

If you go to a café or restaurant, why don't you challenge yourself and at the end ask for the bill in French.

**Useful phrases**

l'addition, s'il vous plaît ....the bill, please

merci ..........................thank you

l'addition, s'il vous plaît

€ 3
€ 5
€ 2
€10

**Challenge achieved**

Tick when completed

## Can I buy a souvenir in French?

When you are on holiday you may see something like a pen or a pencil that may make a nice souvenir of your holiday.
For this challenge, you need to say which souvenir you would like then say
**s'il vous plaît** (please).

un ballon        une gomme        un t-shirt

un crayon

un stylo

un nounours

**Challenge achieved**

Tick when completed

Can I ask for some chocolates in French?

France is well known for it's lovely chocolate, and for this challenge you need to find a shop which sells individual chocolates.

Point at the chocolates you would like, say the quantity you require followed by **s'il vous plaît** (please).
e.g. Quatre, s'il vous plaît (4, please)

Or say the quanity you require, followed by **de ces chocolats, s'il vous plaît.**
e.g.trois de ces chocolats, s'il vous plaît
(3 of these chocolates, please)

deux de ces chocolats, s'il vous plaît
(2 of these chocolates, please)

Remember yes is **oui** and no is **non**.
And thank you is **merci.**

alternative challenge: ask for some crisps:
**des chips, s'il vous plaît**

**Challenge achieved**

Tick when completed

## Can I buy a post card in French?

It can be nice to buy a post card when you are on holiday, either to send to someone or to keep as a souvenir of your holiday. So challenge yourself to buy a post card in French!

Une carte postale, s'il vous plaît
(a post card, please)

**Challenge achieved**

Tick when completed

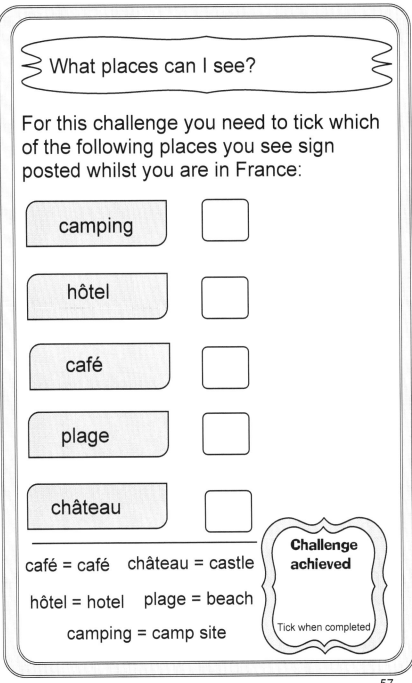

What places can I see?

For this challenge you need to tick which of the following places you see sign posted whilst you are in France:

camping ☐

hôtel ☐

café ☐

plage ☐

château ☐

café = café    château = castle

hôtel = hotel    plage = beach

camping = camp site

**Challenge achieved**

Tick when completed

57

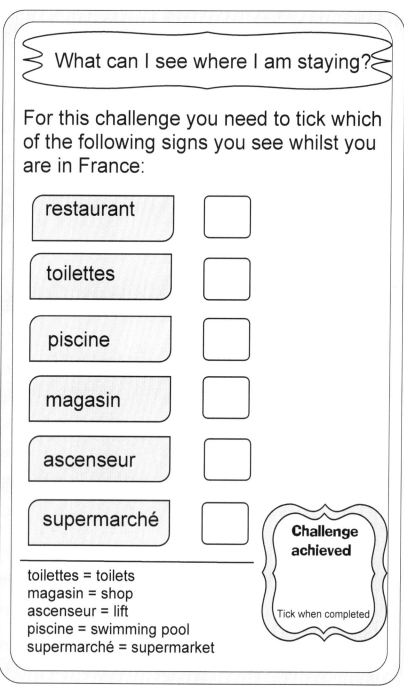

What can I see where I am staying?

For this challenge you need to tick which of the following signs you see whilst you are in France:

restaurant ☐

toilettes ☐

piscine ☐

magasin ☐

ascenseur ☐

supermarché ☐

toilettes = toilets
magasin = shop
ascenseur = lift
piscine = swimming pool
supermarché = supermarket

**Challenge achieved**

Tick when completed

# French　　　　English

| | French | | English |
|---|---|---|---|
| | anglais | | English |
| l' | ascenseur | the | lift |
| | Au revoir | | Good bye |
| une | baguette | a | French stick |
| un | ballon | a | ball |
| une | banane | a | banana |
| les | boissons | the | drinks |
| | Bonjour | | Good day |
| | Bonsoir | | Good evening |
| le | café | the | coffee shop |
| un | café | a | coffee |
| le | camping | the | campsite |
| au | caramel | | caramel |
| une | carte postale | a | post card |
| des | champignons | some | mushrooms |
| le | château | the | castle |
| du | chocolat | some | chocolate |
| | cinq | | five |
| un | citron | a | lemon |
| du | citron | some | lemon |
| un | coca | a | coke |
| un | coca light | a | diet coke |
| | coco | | coconut |
| un | crayon | a | pencil |

| French | | English | |
|---|---|---|---|
| de la | crème | some | cream |
| une | crêpe | a | sweet pancake |
| un | croissant | a | croissant |
| | deux | | two |
| | dix | | ten |
| les | douches | the | showers |
| une | eau minérale | a | mineral water |
| les | Étas Unis | | America |
| | Europe | | Europe |
| une | fraise | a | strawberry |
| des | fraises | some | strawberries |
| | français | | French |
| des | frites | some | chips |
| du | fromage | some | cheese |
| une | galette | a | savoury pancake |
| un | gâteau | a | cake |
| une | glace | an | ice cream |
| une | gomme | a | rubber |
| | grand | | big |
| | Grand Bretagne | | Great Britain |
| un | hamburger | a | hamburger |
| l' | hôtel | the | hotel |
| | huit | | eight |
| du | jambon | some | ham |

# French

# English

| | French | | English |
|---|---|---|---|
| | Je m'appelle… | | My name is … |
| | Je voudrais | | I would like |
| un | jus d'orange | an | orange juice |
| un | kiwi | a | kiwi |
| | lait | | milk |
| une | limonade | a | lemonade |
| le | magasin | the | shop |
| un | manteau | a | coat |
| un | melon | a | melon |
| | menthe | | mint |
| la | mer | the | sea |
| | merci | | thank you |
| | neuf | | nine |
| | noir | | black |
| | non | | no |
| un | nounours | a | teddy |
| les | numéros | | numbers |
| une | orange | an | orange |
| un | Orangina | a | fizzy orange |
| | oui | | yes |
| du | pain | some | bread |
| un | pain au chocolat | | chocolate inside pastry |
| un | pantalon | | trousers |
| | petit | | small |

☆ ★ ☆ ★ ☆  61

| French | | English | |
|---|---|---|---|
| **French** | | **English** | |
| la | piscine | the | swimming pool |
| une | pizza | a | pizza |
| la | plage | the | beach |
| une | poire | a | pear |
| une | pomme | an | apple |
| du | poulet | some | chicken |
| | quatre | | four |
| le | restaurant | the | restaurant |
| de la | salade | some | salad |
| | Salut | | Hi / Bye |
| | sans | | with |
| | sept | | seven |
| | s'il vous plaît | | please |
| | six | | six |
| un | stylo | a | pen |
| du | sucre | some | sugar |
| le | supermarché | the | supermarket |
| un | thé | a | tea |
| un | timbre | a | stamp |
| des | tomates | some | tomatoes |
| | trois | | three |
| un | t-shirt | a | t-shirt |
| | un | | one |
| | vanille | | vanilla |

☆ ★ ☆ ★ ☆

**If you have now been to France, hope you have had a lovely time and that you had a go of speaking French.**

**In the star write how many of the challenges you managed to complete.**

**Hope you enjoyed using this book. Also available are the following:**

Cool Kids Speak French      ISBN 978 1512234954
Cool Kids Speak French book 2     ISBN 978 1515785131
Cool Kids Do Maths in French     ISBN 978 1545051184
Photocopiable Games for teaching French 9781519292902
Le Singe Qui Change De Couleur ISBN 978 1535416498
Un Alien Sur La Terre        ISBN 978 1537272153
Tu as un animal?           ISBN 978 1541032569

Cool Kids Speak Italian       ISBN 978 1511699297
Cool Kids Speak Spanish      ISBN 978 1512234961
Cool Kids Speak German      ISBN 978 1512234985

On Holiday in Spain Cool Kids Speak Spanish   9781530113163
On Holiday in Italy Cool Kids Speak Italian ISBN 9781530113170

© **Joanne Leyland 2016**

23751424R00039

Printed in Great Britain
by Amazon